WORLD MYTHOLOGY

POSEIDON

B. A. Hoena

Consultant:

Dr. Laurel Bowman
Department of Greek and Roman Studies
University of Victoria, British Columbia

Capstone
press

Mankato, Minnesota

Capstone Press
151 Good Counsel Drive, P.O. Box 669, Mankato, Minnesota 56002
http://www.capstonepress.com

Library of Congress Cataloging-in-Publication Data
Hoena, B. A.
Poseidon / by B. A. Hoena.
   p. cm. — (World mythology)
   Summary: An introduction to the character of Poseidon and his roles in Greek
mythology.
   Includes bibliographical references and index.
   ISBN 0-7368-2499-5 (hardcover)
   1. Poseidon (Greek deity)—Juvenile literature. [1. Poseidon (Greek deity) 2. Mythology,
Greek.] I. Title. II. Series: World mythology (Mankato, Minn.)
BL820.N5H64 2004
398.2′0938′01—dc22   2003012976

Editorial Credits
Juliette Peters, series designer; Patrick Dentinger, book designer and illustrator;
   Alta Schaffer, photo researcher; Eric Kudalis, product planning editor

Photo Credits
Art Resource/Erich Lessing, 4, 8, 12; Réunion des Musées Nationaux, cover (statue), 10, 18,
   20 (top)
Bridgeman Art Library/Southampton City Art Gallery, Hampshire, UK, 14, 16
Corbis/Royalty Free, cover (horse), 1, 6
PhotoDisc Inc., 20 (bottom)

TABLE OF CONTENTS

In Walter Crane's painting *Neptune's Horses,* the sea god Neptune (Greek for Poseidon) controls a crashing wave. The wave is shown as horses because the horse is a symbol of the sea god.

POSEIDON

Ancient Greeks and Romans thought the sea was a dangerous place. Crashing waves sank their small wooden ships. Sailors became lost in storms. People even told myths about monsters that roamed the seas. In these stories, sea monsters tore apart ships and ate drowning sailors.

Poseidon (poh-SYE-don) was the Greek god of the sea. In Roman myths, he was called Neptune. People believed Poseidon controlled the crashing waves and the sea monsters. People prayed to him to keep them safe on sea voyages.

Myths say that Poseidon angered easily and punished people who made him mad. One story tells of the Greek hero Odysseus (oh-DISS-ee-uhss) and his long journey home to the island of Ithaca. Odysseus angered Poseidon by blinding his son Polyphemus (pahl-i-FEE-muhss). In revenge, Poseidon raised storms to keep Odysseus from sailing home. Odysseus struggled for 10 years before he could return to Ithaca.

GREEK and ROMAN *Mythical Figures*

Greek Name: **AMPHITRITE**
Roman Name: **SALACIA**
Poseidon's wife

Greek Name: **ATHENA**
Roman Name: **MINERVA**
Goddess of wisdom

Greek Name: **CRONUS**
Roman Name: **SATURN**
Poseidon's father

Greek Name: **HADES**
Roman Name: **PLUTO**
Poseidon's brother and ruler of
the Underworld

Greek Name: **DEMETER**
Roman Name: **CERES**
Goddess of growing things

Greek Name: **ODYSSEUS**
Roman Name: **ULYSSES**
Greek hero from Ithaca

Greek Name: **POLYPHEMUS**
Roman Name: **POLYPHEMUS**
Cyclops who is Poseidon's son

Greek Name: **POSEIDON**
Roman Name: **NEPTUNE**
God of the sea

Greek Name: **RHEA**
Roman Name: **OPS**
Poseidon's mother

Greek Name: **ZEUS**
Roman Name: **JUPITER**
Poseidon's brother and ruler of
the gods

Ancient Greeks and Romans told many types of myths. Creation myths told about the birth of the gods. They also told how the world was created. One creation myth explained how Poseidon became god of the sea.

Explanation myths were another type of myth. These stories helped people explain natural events that they did not understand. Long ago, ancient Greeks and Romans did not know what caused earthquakes. So they told stories to explain earthquakes. People believed the sea held the earth. Poseidon controlled the sea and could shake the earth by stirring up the water. People often called Poseidon "Earthshaker" because they believed that he caused earthquakes.

Explanation myths also told where things came from. One story says Poseidon gave a horse to the city of Athens, Greece. Poseidon wanted the people of Athens to worship him. Poseidon's gift was the world's first horse.

In this ancient sculpture, Rhea hands Cronus a rock wrapped in blankets. Cronus thinks the rock is his son Zeus.

THE OLYMPIANS

Poseidon's parents were giants called **Titans**. His father, the Titan Cronus (KROH-nuhss), ruled the sky and the gods. His mother was the Titaness Rhea (REE-uh). Cronus and Rhea had three sons and three daughters. Their children were all gods.

Cronus worried that his children would grow stronger than he was. He decided to imprison them. Cronus swallowed each child after the child was born. His children did not die. They were **immortal**. Cronus only trapped them in his stomach.

Cronus' actions angered Rhea. So she played a trick on him when their last child, Zeus (ZOOSS), was born. Rhea gave Cronus a rock wrapped in a blanket to eat instead of Zeus.

When Zeus grew up, he helped Poseidon and his other **siblings** escape from Cronus' stomach. The young gods then fled to Mount Olympus in Greece. There, they became known as the **Olympians**. The Olympians did not want Cronus to imprison them again. They planned to **overthrow** Cronus.

On this ancient Greek vase, Poseidon is shown holding the trident that the Cyclopes made for him. Ancient Greeks decorated everyday items like vases, cups, and bowls with scenes from myths.

GOD OF THE SEA

The Olympians knew they needed help to defeat Cronus and the other Titans. Zeus asked the **Cyclopes** (sye-KLOH-peez) to help them. The Cyclopes were one-eyed giants and skilled blacksmiths. They made magic weapons for Zeus, Poseidon, and Hades (HAY-deez). Poseidon received a trident that he could use to control the seas. The magic weapons helped the Olympians defeat the Titans.

Poseidon and his brothers then drew names to see who would rule each part of the world. Zeus' name was picked first. He chose to rule the sky. Poseidon's name was picked next. He chose to rule the sea. Their brother Hades was left with the **Underworld**.

The Olympians chose Zeus to be ruler of the gods because he helped them escape Cronus. Poseidon was not happy that his younger brother could tell him what to do. Poseidon decided not to live with the other gods on Mount Olympus. He lived in an underwater castle off the shore of Greece.

Poseidon (right) and Amphitrite (center) ride their son Triton's (left) tail in this ancient Roman painting.

POSEIDON'S CHILDREN

Poseidon married Amphitrite (am-FI-trye-tee). She was a sea **nymph**. Poseidon and Amphitrite had a son named Triton (TRYE-tuhn). Triton had the upper body of a man and the lower body of a fish.

Poseidon was not a loyal husband. He had several children with other nymphs, women, and goddesses. Poseidon and the sea nymph Thoosa had a son named Polyphemus. Polyphemus was a Cyclops (SYE-klahpss). Poseidon and a woman named Iphimedeia (if-i-MEE-dee-uh) had giant sons called Otus and Ephialtes (eff-i-AL-teez). Otus and Ephialtes often misbehaved. The brothers once tried to reach the heavens by piling three mountains on top of each other.

Like many gods, Poseidon had the power to change himself into an animal. He and the goddess Demeter (dee-MEE-tur) **mated** as horses. Their son was a horse named Arion (uh-RYE-uhn). Arion ran faster than any other horse in the world.

The Death of Medusa by Edward Coley Burne-Jones
shows Perseus after he cut off Medusa's head.

MEDUSA

Poseidon loved a woman named Medusa (mi-DOO-suh). She was very beautiful. Medusa became pregnant with Poseidon's children.

Poseidon and the goddess Athena (uh-THEE-nuh) did not like each other. They often argued. Athena was not strong enough to fight Poseidon. She harmed Medusa instead. Athena turned Medusa into a horrible monster. Medusa grew snakes for hair. People turned to stone when they looked into her eyes.

The Greek hero Perseus (PUR-see-uhss) was sent on a **quest** to kill Medusa. Athena helped Perseus. She gave him a strong sword to kill Medusa. Perseus sneaked up on Medusa, using his shield as a mirror to look at her. In this way, Medusa could not turn him to stone. Perseus then cut off Medusa's head.

When Perseus cut off Medusa's head, her unborn children leapt from her body. Pegasus (PEG-uh-suhss) was a winged horse. Chrysaor (KRIS-ay-or) grew to be a powerful giant.

In *The Doom Fulfilled* by Edward Coley Burne-Jones, Perseus battles the sea monster that Poseidon sent to eat Andromeda.

ANDROMEDA

Perseus headed home with Medusa's head. On his way, he met Princess Andromeda (an-DROM-uh-duh). She was chained to a rock, crying. Perseus stopped to ask her what was wrong.

Queen Cassiopeia (kass-ee-oh-PEE-uh) of Ethiopia was Andromeda's mother. She had told people that Andromeda was more beautiful than Poseidon's sea nymphs. The queen's bragging angered Poseidon. He punished Cassiopeia by sending a sea monster to destroy her kingdom. The kingdom could be saved only if the monster was allowed to eat Andromeda.

Andromeda begged Perseus to save her from the monster. He promised to help Andromeda if she would marry him. She agreed.

Perseus met Poseidon's sea monster as it rose from the water. He jumped on it, cutting and slashing it with his sword. The sea turned red from the monster's blood. After a long fight, the monster died. Perseus freed Andromeda and then married her.

Antoine-Louis Barye's sculpture *Theseus and the Minotaur* shows the Greek hero Theseus fighting the Minotaur.

THE MINOTAUR

When Minos (MY-nohss) became king of Crete, he prayed to Poseidon. Minos asked the sea god for a large bull. This gift would show Minos' enemies that Poseidon supported the king. Minos promised to **sacrifice** the bull in honor of Poseidon.

Poseidon sent Minos a large white bull. Minos thought the bull was too beautiful to kill. He decided to keep it. Poseidon was angry that Minos broke his promise. So Poseidon played a trick on the king. He made Minos' wife, Pasiphaë (pa-SIF-ay-ee), fall in love with the bull. Pasiphaë and the bull had a child. It was called the Minotaur (MIN-uh-tor). The Minotaur had the lower body of a man and the upper body of a bull.

Daedalus (DED-uh-luhss) was a wise man who worked for King Minos. He made a cage for the Minotaur. This cage was a large maze. Only Daedalus knew the way out of the maze. Years later, Poseidon's son Theseus (THEE-see-uhss) sailed to Crete. He entered the maze and killed the Minotaur.

Rene-Antoine Houasse's painting (above) shows Poseidon making the first horse. The planet Neptune (right) is named using Poseidon's Roman name.

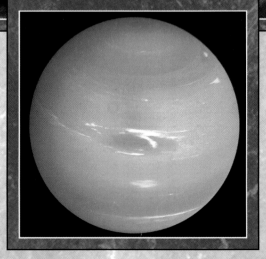

MYTHOLOGY TODAY

Greek and Roman myths still influence the world. The planets in our solar system are named after Roman gods. Neptune is the Roman name for Poseidon. It is also the name for the eighth planet in our solar system.

People use names from myths for other things. Both the USS *Poseidon* and USS *Neptune* were names of U.S. Navy ships. Neptune is the name of a town in New Jersey.

Today, people no longer believe that Greek and Roman myths are true. Instead, they use science to explain events like earthquakes. But people still tell myths. Myths are exciting and enjoyable stories. The story of Perseus killing Medusa is a popular myth. The killing of the Minotaur by Theseus is another popular story. Not only are myths exciting stories, but they also help people understand ancient cultures. Myths show what people believed long ago.

Adriatic Sea

•Rome

ITALY

GREECE

Aegean Sea

•Troy

ITHACA

Thebes
•

Ionian Sea

Athens

SICILY

Sparta

CRETE

SCALE
Miles
0   100   200

0   100   200
Kilometers

KEY
• City
⛰ Mount Olympus

Mediterranean Sea

GLOSSARY

ancient (AYN-shunt)—having lived long ago

Cyclopes (sye-KLOH-peez)—giants with one eye in the middle of their foreheads

immortal (i-MOR-tuhl)—able to live forever

mate (MATE)—to join together to produce young

nymph (NIMF)—a female spirit or goddess found in a meadow, a forest, a mountain, a sea, or a stream

Olympian (oh-LIM-pee-uhn)—one of 12 powerful gods who lived on Mount Olympus in Greece

overthrow (oh-vur-THROH)—to defeat and remove a leader from power

quest (KWEST)—a journey taken by a hero to perform a task

sacrifice (SAK-ruh-fisse)—to give up something to honor a god

sibling (SIB-ling)—a brother or a sister

Titan (TYE-ten)—one of 12 giants who ruled the world before the Olympians

Underworld (UHN-dur-wurld)—the place under the ground where spirits of the dead go

READ MORE

Green, Jen. *Myths of Ancient Greece.* Mythic World. Austin, Texas: Raintree Steck-Vaughn, 2001.

Hoena, B. A. *Cyclopes.* World Mythology. Mankato, Minn.: Capstone Press, 2004.

USEFUL ADDRESSES

National Junior Classical League
422 Wells Mill Drive
Miami University
Oxford, OH 45056

Ontario Classical Association
P.O. Box 19505
55 Bloor Street West
Toronto, ON M4W 1A5
Canada

INTERNET SITES

FactHound offers a safe, fun way to find Internet sites related to this book. All of the sites on FactHound have been researched by our staff.

Here's how:
1. Visit *www.facthound.com*
2. Type in this special code **0736824995** for age-appropriate sites. Or enter a search word related to this book for a more general search.
3. Click on the **Fetch It** button.

FactHound will fetch the best sites for you!

INDEX